CONTENTS

SAINT WENCESLAUS

ALSO KNOWN AS GOOD KING WENCESLAS

A SHORT INTRODUCTION

By Jan Rejzl

1st Choice Publishing

Great Britain

ISBN 978-0-9527339-2-8

Dedicated to my grandchildren:
Jude, Rufus, Joseph & Idris

1. ORIGINS OF WENCESLAUS'S NAME

In the Old Czech Language his name was Wenceslav meaning Great Glory. And Wenceslaus is the Latin version which was adopted as the English version of his name in the USA and Canada. It was also true in England as I came across a certain Wenceslaus Hollar (1607-1677), a prolific engraver in that country.

The writer John Mason Neal may have changed his name to Wenceslas for his Christmas carol *'Good King Wenceslas'* and this is of course how Wenceslaus is better known in England now. In the Czech Language it is now Vaclav. In Russian, when translated from the Cyrillic script it is Viatcheslav. In this book I will be using his name as Wenceslaus.

When it comes to his title, in some texts, he is Prince while in Latin he was referred to as "Rex" which can be translated as "King" or "leader" of a nation or region. In the Czech Language he was referred to as Duke once he ascended to the throne.

2. ORIGINS OF HIS TRIBE AND NATION

When the Slavs moved to the Bohemian basin, they came in as tribes, family related groups of people. Wenceslaus's tribe was called the Czechs. They settled in the centre of Bohemia. From legends we learn about Duchess Libuse founding the Premyslid ruling dynasty of dukes and later kings who at first ruled central Bohemia then expanded their influence to the whole of Bohemia, and later on Moravia, to form the Czech Kingdom, which very much covers the present day Czech Republic.

The first historically substantiated Czech ruler was Wenceslaus's grandfather Borivoj. Borivoj married his wife Ludmila when she was young, 15 years of age. By that marriage Borivoj added the area around Melnik which was ruled by her father. Borivoj was christened by Greek missionaries on his visit to Moravia in around 874. Borivoj and Ludmila had two sons: Spitihnev and Vratislav, Spitihnev being the elder son. Both sons were brought up as Christians.

Borivoj died at the age of 36 while his sons were still very young. Svatopluk of Moravia took direct rule over the Czech Dukedom. Svatopluk was married to Borivoj's sister and the rule was conferred on him by Arnulf, Duke of Bavaria. In 894, Svatopluk died leaving Spitihnev to take over at the age of 19.

Spitihnev too helped Christianity to spread and built a new church in Budec dedicated to Saint Peter. Budec became the first seat of learning in Central Bohemia. Spitihnev built additional castles on the borders of his dukedom like the one on the river

Elbe in today's Stara Boleslav.

Vratislav, the younger of the two brothers, father of Wenceslaus, assumed a secondary role under his brother's rule. He went on diplomatic and military missions. On one of the missions to another Slavic dukedom called Stodor, further north in what is now Germany, he met his future wife Drahomira. Although the Stodor people were pagan at that time, it is assumed that Drahomira was christened before they got married.

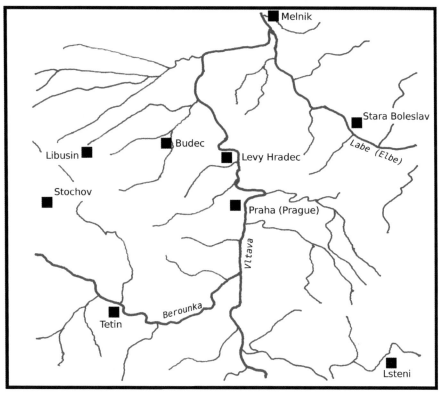

Fig.1 Central Bohemia at the time of Wenceslaus.

3. BIRTH AND EDUCATION OF WENCESLAUS

Wenceslaus was born at the beginning of the 10th Century in around 907. We have not got a precise date, as few records were kept in those days.

There is a legend, that he was born in Stochov, where his grand-mother Ludmila planted an oak tree when he was born. The legend further says that the nannies watered the sapling with Wenceslaus's bath water giving the tree extra staying powers and the tree is still there today. The name of the place Stochov in the Czech Language now means 'hundred nannies'.

Fig. 2 Duchess Ludmila planting the oak tree while Wence-slaus's parents Drahomira and Vratislav look on holding baby Wenceslaus.

The tree is still there today, as can be seen in the next picture. The tree trunk was held together by steel rings and there were branches with green leaves when I first visited Stochov in 1988.

The dead tree branches were cut down and the tree looks now

like the picture below taken in 2016. There is a statue of St Wenceslaus in front of the tree now.

Fig.3 The Oak tree in 2016.

A church dedicated to Saint Wenceslaus was built there in front of the tree and you can see the interior and exterior of the church in fig. 4.

Fig.4 Saint Wenceslaus church in Stochov

There are no written records where and exactly when he was born. Some argue that he may have been born in the castle on the river Elbe, where Stara Boleslav is today.

With the arrival of Christianity also came writing. The Germanic missionaries used Latin while in Moravia, east of Bohemia, the Greek missionaries later known as Saints Cyril and

Methodius brought with them new writing developed by Saint Cyril known as Glagolitic Script.

At first, Christianity came to Bohemia from Moravia with the Christening of Borivoj in Moravia in around 874. Borivoj brought back with him a Slavic priest called Kaich and built the first church of stone and mortar in Bohemia. He dedicated it to Saint Clement, in his main seat of residence and rule at that time which was the castle of Levy Hradec. You can see the location of Levy Hradec in the map in figure 1.

We know from the remaining foundations of this church in Levy Hradec that it was a rotunda, similar to the one pictured on the front cover of this book.

After Borivoj's death, his widow Duchess Ludmila had a Slavic priest with her called Paul. So from him Wenceslaus would have learned the Slavic writing in Glagolitic Script.

Fig.5 Duchess Ludmila with young Wenceslaus and her priest Paul.

Also, during the times of Wenceslaus there was a school established in the castle Budec, where Latin writing and reading were taught. This is where his father sent him when he was older.

Latin was already an important religious and diplomatic language. In Budec, they used boards or slates covered with wax on which they would engrave their writing. These implements were found during archaeological excavations in Budec. There was a smaller church there dedicated to Saint Peter, foundations of which were found in today's larger church there.

All the legends agree that Wenceslaus was a gifted pupil and could soon read religious books in Latin as well as any priest could.

His grandmother Ludmila, a devout Christian herself, taught him the importance of true faith in God and Christianity.

Young Wenceslaus helped with harvesting the corn and making wine for use in Christian communion.

Fig.6 Young Wenceslaus helping with harvesting corn and making wine in a painting in Saint Wenceslaus Basilica in Stara Boleslav.

Young Wenceslaus was also taught how to ride a horse and handle sword and lance. Wenceslaus's father ascended the ducal throne when Wenceslaus was 8 years old. So, from that age as the oldest son of the Duke, the military education would have been as important as learning Latin. Wenceslaus in his adulthood proved to be unafraid to go into battle. He had two brothers, of whom only Boleslav outlived him, while Wenceslaus's other younger brother died young. Wenceslaus also had four sisters.

Fig. 7 Young Wenceslaus learning to handle a sword.

4. HIS FATHER'S REIGN

Wenceslaus's uncle, Duke Spytihnev, died aged 40 leaving no heir. Wenceslaus' father Vratislav then ascended the ducal throne in 915. Duke Vratislav then moved with his wife and children to Prague Castle. Vratislav built there a second church dedicated to Saint George, which was later rebuilt into a larger basilica dedicated to Saint George which is still there today.

At this time, a major ritual took place celebrating the cutting of the hair of the growing Prince Wenceslaus. Special celebration of the cutting of the hair was originally a pagan ritual, known in the east as well as in the west and adopted by the church. The ritual took place twice, once at an early age and once when the child passed from the exclusive care of the mother to supervision by the father.

The happy childhood of Wenceslaus was shattered when his father Duke Vratislav died suddenly in 920. It is not known how he died, but it is assumed by historians that his death occurred in a battle defending his country.

Wenceslaus was only 13 years old at that time. He, as the oldest male, was expected to become the duke. The ceremony was performed in Prague Castle in front of Saint George's Church. When people assembled, he was seated on the duke's stone throne. The legends say that from that moment his younger brother Boleslav was expected to do as Wenceslaus told him.

It was decided by the elders that his mother Drahomira would rule on his behalf. However, she was not given full powers and she was obliged to confer and to take advice from her mother-in-law, Ludmila. Ludmila was also entrusted with overseeing the education and upbringing of the two princes, Wenceslaus and Boleslav.

5. DRAHOMIRA'S RULE

Drahomira resented taking advice from Ludmila and the fact that Ludmila was entrusted with overseeing her two sons' upbringing. Ludmila was aware of Drahomira's resentment of her and moved to Tetin, a castle with estates. But that was not enough and Drahomira sent two assassins to Tetin and they strangled her on 16 September 921.

There has not been much written about Drahomira's rule in the early legends and people and writers tried to fill in this period much later. Drahomira came from a Slavic tribe which was at that time pagan and stayed that way for many years after. So, it was assumed that she turned back to her pagan ways and surrounded herself with the people sympathetic to those ways. Bohemia was at that time half pagan and half Christian and the old pagan ways were still surviving. It is believed that she further suppressed Christianity. There was pressure on young Wenceslaus, as their young duke, to abandon his Christian ways and beliefs and to join in pagan ceremonies and feasts.

However, Wenceslaus stayed faithful to Christianity and very often prayed at night, secretly inviting those Christian priests left in the country to join him.

Ludmila was buried in Tetin and people came to her grave and prayed there. She had been known for her pious life and soon people reported miracles happening near her grave. Drahomira had a small wooden church built over the grave, and dedicated to Saint Michael, so that any miracles or special heavenly signs happening there could be attributed to Saint Michael and not to the blessed Ludmila.

During the rule of Drahomira, in 922, Arnulf, Duke of Bavaria, invaded Bohemia with his army. The Czech army, with the young Duke Wenceslaus in front, then about a 15-year-old boy, went to meet them in the border region. There are no detailed reports about the purpose or the outcome of this military encounter. It is believed that the relationship between Bavaria and Bohemia stayed unchanged.

6. WENCESLAUS'S YEARS OF REIGN

In around 925, Wenceslaus at the age of 18 took power and started to rule on his own. Christianity survived in peoples' hopes, but the pagan opposition to it gained strength under his mother's rule too.

Wenceslaus assembled all the noblemen and elders and told them that never again must anybody be denied the freedom to learn about Jesus Christ's teachings and to be a Christian. But this firm stand polarised the two camps and blood spilled. Wenceslaus called the noblemen again and said to them that he would rule under Christian principles but at same time he would uphold the most punitive laws of the land.

Wenceslaus brought the body of his beloved grandmother Ludmila from Tetin to Prague Castle on 21st October 925, and she was buried in Saint George's church with all honours. People remembered her Christian ways and her martyrdom and frequently came to her grave and prayed to her. She was officially canonised about 200 years later.

Legends say that Wenceslaus built many churches out of wood. This was an easily obtainable material from which people built their homes. Even the civil buildings at the Prague Castle were built of wood at that time. But there was one church he built with stone in Prague Castle and we have records of it.

Building with stone and mortar was a new way to build in Bohemia and it is believed that master craftsmen had to be brought in from abroad. Originally it was going to be dedicated to Saint Emmeram but later it was dedicated to Saint Vitus.

In 929 King Henry the Fowler of Saxony and Duke Arnulf of Bavaria marched together into Bohemia with a huge army. Wenceslaus, rather than fighting a losing battle, chose to follow his predecessors and pay tribute for the alliance annually, believed to be in silver and cattle. Such payments were customary in those days and Saxony made payments to the newly settled Magyar horsemen to stop their raids into Bavaria and Saxony. Bohemia benefited from this agreement too.

In some of the later legends it is said that Wenceslaus attended Saxony's assembly after 929, thought to be in today's Aachen. It is believed that at that time he would have been given Saint Vitus relics so he could dedicate his church, a sophisticated rotunda in its time, to Saint Vitus.

Fig.8 Artistic reconstruction of how Saint Vitus Rotunda may have looked.

Over the centuries, Wenceslaus's rotunda of Saint Vitus was rebuilt into a basilica, and then into a cathedral. The original foundations of St. Vitus Rotunda were found underneath the floor of today's Saint Wenceslaus Chapel in the Saint Vitus Cathedral.

Fig.9 Ground layout of Saint Vitus Rotunda, Saint Vitus Basilica and Saint Vitus Cathedral, showing the original Rotunda in black and the basilica in red – both replaced by the current cathedral in blue.

One heroic act of Duke Wenceslaus is known to us from the legends, when he put the lives of his soldiers and those of the enemy soldiers before his own life. According to this legend a neighbouring duke, Radslav of Kourim, tried to extend his rule over Wenceslaus's dukedom. He started to provoke Wenceslaus by unfriendly actions and soon the two armies of both dukedoms were marching against each other.

Wenceslaus tried to save the lives of soldiers on both sides by asking Radslav to meet him in a man-to-man duel. There are no detailed reports about the encounter. The later legend says that Radslav saw a picture of the Holy Cross on Wenceslaus's forehead and at once realised that if God was on his enemy's side that he would not be able to overcome the man. He threw his sword aside and knelt before Wenceslaus. Wenceslaus added Radslav's dukedom to his but spared Radslav's life and asked him to look after it for him.

We now know that Wenceslaus was in battles during his life because his skull, which is kept today in the Saint Vitus Cathedral, has wounds on it which must have been inflicted during his life as they have healed.

Wenceslaus lived and ruled like a true Christian, which may not always have been easy. Later legends after his death talk about it very vividly. They say that he sat on trials to ensure they were fair and that he visited prisoners and tried to educate them in Christian ways of life. In the following painting in the Saint Wenceslaus Basilica in Stara Boleslav, he is depicted helping young and destitute children.

Fig. 10 Wenceslaus is buying children out of slavery (on the right) and providing shelter and education for orphans (on the left)

7. DOMESTIC MATTERS FOR WENCESLAUS

His younger brother Boleslav looked after the eastern part of the dukedom for Wenceslaus. It was even referred to by some writers as Boleslavia. Boleslav was overly ambitious as we can see later from his actions, and he surrounded himself with Wenceslaus's enemies. The tribute to King Henry the Fowler had to be collected from the whole of the country and, obviously, it was not popular with some people.

Boleslav had a church dedicated to Saints Cosmas and Damian in his castle and employed a priest. We cannot, therefore, just simply assume that it was resentment of Wenceslaus's rule with Christian principles to blame for what happened next.

Boleslav invited Wenceslaus to his castle on the river Elbe in today's Stara Boleslav for the celebration of the feast of Saints Cosmas and Damian, then falling on Sunday 27 September. Duke Wenceslaus customarily visited churches on their feast days, so he did not find it at all suspicious.

Wenceslaus had not intended to stay overnight with his company, and he wanted to leave after the religious ceremony. However, he was persuaded by Boleslav to stay overnight. So, in the afternoon they all saddled horses and both Wenceslaus's and Boleslav's knights joined in games in the court of Boleslav' castle.

Once evening reception was over, Wenceslaus prayed into the night as he always did. In the morning he hastened to the church of Saints Cosmas and Damian for his morning prayers.

Outside, he was stopped by his brother Boleslav. After a brief exchange of words, it is believed, Boleslav drew his sword against Wenceslaus. Wenceslaus was experienced in combat and managed to deflect Boleslav's blow so only his ear was cut. He manged to wrestle Boleslav to the ground, but when another of Boleslav's men attacked Wenceslaus, Wenceslaus realised he was outnumbered and ran to the church as a place of sanctuary. But the door was locked, and Boleslav's accomplices killed him at the door. According to the First Slavonic Legend, Wenceslaus died instantly.

Afterwards, Boleslav sent his soldiers to Prague Castle to eliminate Wenceslaus's supporters. Wenceslaus's body was buried next to the church in Boleslav's castle.

The murder shocked the Czech people and the news of it travelled widely across Europe. It was written about in the First Slavonic Legend. The year and date of his death is now recognised as 28th September 935. It used to be shown as 28th September 929, but that error may have been introduced when the First Slavonic Legend was transcribed from Glagolitic script to Cyrillic writing. The year 935 fits also with other historical data as shown later.

8. TIMES AFTER WENCESLAUS

Boleslav moved his residence to Prague Castle to rule from there over the whole dukedom. The situation in Bohemia was unsettled for some time as Boleslav had to secure allegiance from Wenceslaus's supporters.

On the wider European scene, King Henry the Fowler of Saxony suffered a stroke in the autumn of 935 and died in 936 and thus could not interfere in Bohemia after Wenceslaus's death in 935. Henry's son Otto I entered a war with Boleslav which lasted 14 years, until he had to agree to pay tribute to Otto in 950.

It may have been this state of war Boleslav was in, and the fact that kind rule of Wenceslaus was not forgotten by the Czech people, that he had Wenceslaus's body transferred from his castle in Stara Boleslav to Prague Castle and reburied in the Saint Vitus Rotunda on Sunday 4th March 938. On the orders of Boleslav this was done at night.

The transfer of Wenceslaus's body to Prague Castle proved popular with Czech people.

Boleslav repented his act against his brother and sent his younger daughter Mlada to Rome with a plea for the establishment of an independent bishopric in Prague but that was only achieved after his death in 972.

The Prague bishopric was established in 973 by Boleslav's son Boleslav II, who became the ruling duke. Boleslav II, also called "Boleslav the Religious", established the first convent in Bohemia, attached to Saint George's church in Prague Castle, and his sister Mlada became the first abbess.

The first bishop of Prague was Deitmar, a Saxon priest, who spent a considerable time in Bohemia and could speak Czech. The second bishop, Vojtech, was of princely Bohemian birth.

9. GROWING RESPECT FOR WENCESLAUS

The beloved Duke Wenceslaus was remembered by his people for his Christian ways and kind rule. People prayed to him and talked about miracles happening in his name. It is believed that he was canonised by the first or second bishop of Prague.

The celebration of Saint Wenceslaus's feast on September 28th started sometimes after the transfer of his body to Prague Castle. He became the first Czech saint and patron of the Czech Dukedom and later Czech Kingdom. It is now a public holiday in the Czech Republic.

There were churches built and dedicated to him in Bohemia, Moravia and also centuries later in North America by the Czech settlers there. Saint Wenceslaus appeared on coins in Bohemia from 11th century up to the present days of Czech Republic.

It is believed that the second bishop of Prague, Vojtech, composed a song dedicated to Saint Wenceslaus. This became the anthem of Czech Dukedom and the later Czech Kingdom. Indeed it remained so until 28th October 1918, when Czechoslovakia was formed as a republic from the Czech Kingdom and Slovakia, a Slavic part of the Hungarian Kingdom.

10. ENGLISH CHRISTMAS CAROL

We must not forget the Christmas Carol 'Good King Wenceslas looked out', composed by John Mason Neal who was born in London 1818. In 1836 he won an open scholarship to Trinity College, Cambridge. He took his degree in Theology in 1840 and stayed in the college as lecturer. He also shone there as a poet and won several prizes for sacred poems.

In the spring of 1846, he became a warden of Sackville College in East Grinstead, an old people's home, established there in 1608 by the Earl of Dorset. The post gave him plenty of time to write and he wrote many books, hymns and carols, among them 'Good King Wenceslas', published in 1853. Sackville College still functions today as an old people's home and its grounds are open to visitors in summer months.

The tune for the carol was taken from an old spring carol published in a book in 1582 for the Lutheran Communion in Sweden.

The words are by John Mason Neal: -

Good King Wenceslas

1.   "Good King Wenceslas looked out
On the feast of Stephen
When the snow lay round about
Deep and Crisp and even."
"Brightly shone the moon that night
though the frost was cruel,
When a poor man came in sight,
Gath 'ring winter fuel."

2.   "Hither, page, and stand by me,
If thou know'st it, telling
Yonder peasant, who is he?
Where, and what his dwelling?"
"Sire, he lives a good league hence,
Underneath the mountain;
Right against the forest fence,
By St Agnes fountain."

3.   "Bring me flesh and bring me wine,
Bring me pine logs thither;
Thou and I will see him dine,
When we bear them hither."
"Page and monarch forth they went,
Onward both together,
Through the rude winds wild lament
And the bitter weather."

4.   "Sire, the night is darker now
And the wind blows stronger;
Fails my heart, I know not how,
I can go no longer."
"Mark my footsteps, good my page!

Tread thou in them boldly;
Thou shall find the winter's rage
Freeze thy blood less coldly."

5.   "In his master's steps he trod,
Where the snow lay dinted;
Heat was in the very sod
Which the saint had printed.
Therefore, Christian men, be sure -
Wealth or rank possessing -
Ye, who now will bless the poor,
Shall yourselves find blessing. "

The carol is based on the good deeds written about Saint Wenceslaus once his respect was well established, some years after his death. The following painting in the Saint Wenceslaus Basilica in Stara Boleslav relates to the carol.

Fig.11 Wenceslaus delivering wood to a widow with his page Podevin following in his footsteps.

11. PLACES OF INTEREST

The two most important places in our story are Prague and Stara Boleslav.

Prague's hilly left bank of the river Vltava was inhabited first because the right-hand bank suffered from flooding by the river.

The early buildings were of wood as wood was freely available. Building with stone and mortar only arrived with Christianity. The first such buildings were the church of Saint Clement in Levy Hradec and the second was Saint Mary's church at Prague Castle, both built by Duke Borivoj.

We know the early boundaries of Prague Castle from archaeological excavation. But the early internal layout of the first wooden buildings was lost by continuous rebuilding of the castle. The first walls may have been of wood and soil with dry stone facing. The area of the castle stayed the same from then till today because of the terrain constrains.

An artist's painting in fig. 12 shows the layout of Prague Castle some years after it's establishment, once the walls were of stone and the 3 stone churches of St Mary, St Vitus and St George with the adjacent Convent were added.

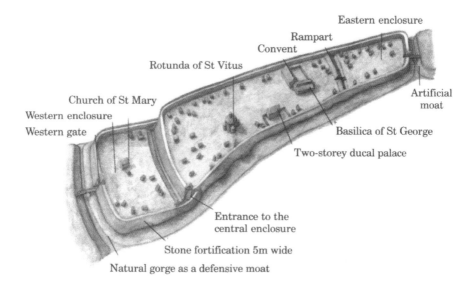

Fig.12 Prague Castle in the late 10th Century (by L. Anlauf)

Fig. 13 Prague Castle today with St. Vitus Cathedral in the middle.

In Saint Vitus Cathedral there is a chapel called Saint Wenceslaus Chapel. This contains a statue of Saint Wenceslaus, which is some 2 meters tall. It is believed that the sculptor had access to his skull and bones as his grave was opened at that time in 1373. In the not so distant past the head profile of the statue was projected against his skull and they matched. So, it is believed that this statue is the closest depiction of him we have today. You may have noticed the hat he is wearing in paintings and statues. It is unique and it is the Czech Ducal Hat symbolising that he is the Duke of the Czech Lands.

Fig. 14 Statue of Saint Wenceslaus in Saint Vitus Cathedral.

The castle in Stara Boleslav guarded a widely used crossing of the river Elbe on an important route east from Prague to Poland.

Ever since Wenceslaus was killed there and declared a Saint, it became the number one pilgrimage site in Bohemia. Later on, the Basilica of Saint Wenceslaus was erected above the place of his martyrdom by Duke Bretislav and was consecrated on 18 May 1046. It was first built in the Romanesque style, but there are no images depicting the Basilica in this style as it was later rebuilt.

Fig. 15 Basilica of Saint Wenceslaus on the right, built over the church of Saints Cosmas and Damian, now represented by a crypt. On the left is a small Romanesque church dedicated to Saint Clement.

The Royal Castle in Stara Boleslav was burnt out in the Hussites Wars in about 1433 and never rebuilt. The grounds since then are being used by the church and civilians as accommodation.

There is another church in Stara Boleslav dedicated to The
Assumption of The Virgin Mary. It was built where a metal
Madonna was unearthed which is believed to have belonged
to Saint Wenceslaus. It strengthened the importance of Stara
Boleslav as a place of Christian worship and pilgrimage.

*Fig. 16 Church of the Assumption of the Virgin Mary in
Stara Boleslav*

12. WANTING TO LEARN MORE?

My original book 'Good King Wenceslas – The Real Story' offers a lot more information on the subject and places of interest and can be obtained from our websites: https://wenceslaus.net and https://wenceslas.co.uk - the websites only differ in the name and spelling of the saint's name. You can order the book from either of these websites. £9.99 plus reduced postage and packing to UK and worldwide. We look forward to hearing from you.

APPENDIX A - ABOUT THE AUTHOR

I was born in Bohemia which is in Central Europe and is now part of the Czech Republic, in the town called Brandys Nad Labem Stara Boleslav formed from joining two towns: Brandys Nad Labem and Stara Boleslav on opposite banks of the river Elbe (Labe in Czech). Under that name you can find it on a map when you travel east from Prague (Praha in Czech).

I grew up in Stara Boleslav with its basilica dedicated to Saint Wenceslaus where I took my first communion. You can see me on that day in the picture in fig. 17 at the age of 6, in the grounds of Saint Wenceslaus Basilica. I soon became an altar boy there and was one well into my early teens.

Fig. 17 The author at the age of 6 (1954) outside the grounds of Saint Wenceslaus Basilica

I learned the story of Saint Wenceslaus from an early age. When I came to England in 1968 as a 20 year old student for a summer holiday to learn English, I was able to tell my English friends more about Saint Wenceslaus who was known in England from the well-known Christmas carol 'Good King Wenceslas' composed by John Mason Neal and published in 1853.

I left Czechoslovakia for England for good in 1969 and this is where I live now. It was not until I returned to Stara Boleslav in 1988 for a holiday, that I started to research the subject more and then published my first book on the subject in 1995 called: 'Good King Wenceslas – The Real Story'. When talking about

Saint Wenceslaus to my friends in England, they all knew the Christmas carol but did not know that Wenceslaus really existed. That was what made me add 'The Real Story' to the title of that book.

APPENDIX B - EARLY HISTORY OF BOHEMIA

The first identified culture was the Celtic Culture, which spans across Europe from Scotland to Bohemia in one direction and as wide as from parts of France to the Low Countries. The very name of Bohemia is derived from a Celtic tribe called Boi (Boj in Czech) residing around today's Prague. Bohemia means in German 'homeland of the Boi people'.

The Celtic tribes fell to the Germanic tribes during the 1st century BC. The Slavic tribes came from east and north into the Bohemian basin in the 5th century AD. Obviously, the cultures can only be identified by the archaeology associated with them. The Slavic people and their language originated from the region of Europe that is now part of Russia. The Czech Language which is spoken today in Bohemia is a Slavic Language.

Printed in Great Britain
by Amazon

73035887R10024